Forged

Prayer Journal

Unless otherwise indicated, Scripture quotations taken from the New American Standard Bible® (NASB), Copyright © 1960, 1962, 1963, 1968, 1971, 1972, 1973, 1975, 1977, 1995 by The Lockman Foundation Used by permission. www.Lockman.org

Copyright © 2020 Danielle Downing-Hadley.

All rights reserved. No part of this publication may be reproduced, distributed, or transmitted in any form or by any means, including photocopying, recording, or other electronic or mechanical methods, without the prior written permission of the publisher, except in the case of brief quotations embodied in critical reviews and certain other noncommercial uses permitted by copyright law. For permission requests, write to the publisher, addressed at the e-mail address below.

ISBN: 978-1-7353608-1-2 (Paperback)

Bookcover design by Danielle J Mitchell.

Printed by DiggyPOD, Inc., in the United States of America.

First printing edition 2020.

Danielle Downing-Hadley
ddowninghadley@yahoo.com

Welcome to the FORGE !

This work is designed to guide your prayer time as you journey to spiritual refinement. This prayer journal can be used independently or alongside the Forged devotional. Praying with clarity and focus is a foundational step in the refinement process. Each day will begin a scripture followed by a series of refection questions and ending with a personal prayer. This prayer journal is to be a record of your continual time in God's refinery.

Week 1

What kind of metal?

Day 1

You did not choose Me but I chose you and appointed you that you would go and bear fruit and that your fruit would remain, so that whatever you ask of the Father in My name He may give to you.

John 15:16

You are chosen by God. What does this mean to you?

____

____

____

____

____

How does being chosen by God this you feel?

____

____

____

____

____

What are three qualities that you possess that can be used to glorify God?

____

____

____

____

____

What "fruit" do you wish to present to the Lord?

What hinders you from baring fruit?

What do you hear the Lord saying about your ability to bear fruit in this season?

Lord, you have chosen me? Lord you have chosen me. Indeed, Lord you have chosen me! My response to this is...

My Prayer

Day 2

There is no one who calls on Your name, Who arouses himself to take hold of You; For You have hidden Your face from us. And have delivered us into the power of our iniquities. But now, O LORD, You are our Father, We are the clay, and You our potter; And all of us are the work of Your hand.

Isaiah 64:7-8

What are the qualities of a good father?

____

____

____

____

How is God Father to you?

____

____

____

____

List three ways you are being molded by God.

____

____

____

____

How are you being shaped during this season?

____

____

____

What is your relationship to God as the Potter?

____

____

____

Where have you resisted being molded?

____

____

____

Your are the Work of God's hand. Describe how this makes you feel.

____

____

____

____

Take a moment to release your resistance and submit to His process of refinement. Be honest with God about your fears, your insecurities, and your frustrations. Let this motivate and guide your prayer.

My Prayer

Day 3

Blessed be the God and Father of our Lord Jesus Christ, who has blessed us with every spiritual blessing in the heavenly places in Christ, just as He chose us in Him before the foundation of the world, that we would be holy and blameless before Him. In love…

Ephesian 1:1-4

Define the word: Blessed

____

____

____

____

Define the word: Holy

____

____

____

____

Define the word: Blameless

____

____

____

____

What does it mean to be chosen before the foundation of the world?

____

____

____

____

Define spiritual blessings.

____

____

____

What spiritual blessings do you see unfolding in your life?

____

____

____

What spiritual blessings do you seek?

____

____

____

Love is essential to experiencing God as the one who is the source of all blessings. Take a moment to sit in the quiet and reflect on God's love.

My Prayer

Day 4

For by grace you have been saved through faith; and that not of yourselves, it is the gift of God; not as a result of works, so that no one may boast. For we are His workmanship, created in Christ Jesus for good works, which God prepared beforehand so that we would walk in them.

Ephesians 2:8-10

How is grace a gift?

____

____

____

____

____

What is the difference between a gift and a reward?

____

____

____

____

____

In what ways have you tried to earn the grace of God?

____

____

____

____

You were created in Jesus Christ for good works. List the works you feel called or motivated to complete.

____

____

____

____

How are you prepared for the work you have been called to in this season?

____

____

____

____

You have been selected, crafted, and prepared for a great work in Christ Jesus. You have all that you need yet faith is required. Take a moment to acknowledge areas that require faith and grace during this season of refinement.

My Prayer

Day 5

For I know the plans that I have for you,' declares the Lord, 'plans for welfare and not for calamity to give you a future and a hope. Then you will call upon Me and come and pray to Me, and I will listen to you. You will seek Me and find Me when you search for Me with all your heart.

Jeremiah 29:11-13

How has the Lord illustrated His plans for your life? List 3 specific examples.

1.____

____

____

____

2.____

____

____

____

3.____

____

____

____

How does submission to God's plan in difficult times increase faith?

In what ways are you seeking the Lord during this season?

What do you hope your searching reveals?

How do you know that the Lord listens to your prayers?

Searching for the Lord with your all your heart requires intention. Take a moment now to come to the Lord with and open mind and open heart.

My Prayer

Day 6

"But He knows the way I take; When He has tried me, I shall come forth as gold. "My foot has held fast to His path; I have kept His way and not turned aside.

Job 23:10-11

What is the relationship between comfort and complacency?

____

____

____

How do you respond to the Lord pulling you out of your comfort zone?

____

____

____

____

In what areas of your life have you sensed the testing of God?

____

____

____

____

What role does testing have in your relationship with God?

___

___

___

How are you holding your feet to the path and direction of God during this time?

___

___

___

Where have you seen the benefit of discomfort in your refinement process?

___

___

___

The Lord affirms that He know the way that you take. What evidence do you have from your own life?

___

___

___

He knows the way that I take...

My Prayer

Day 7

...fixing our eyes on Jesus, the author and perfecter of faith, who for the joy set before Him endured the cross, despising the shame, and has sat down at the right hand of the throne of God.
Hebrews 12:2

Fix your eyes on Jesus. What do you see?

____

____

____

Define Jesus as the Author.

____

____

____

Define Jesus and the Perfecter.

____

____

____

Define Jesus as Friend.

____

____

____

Define Jesus as King.

____

____

____

____

What is the relationship between joy and the cross?

____

____

____

____

How are you growing in faith as you are being perfected?

____

____

____

____

Imagine walking with Jesus. Imagine Him laughing and smiling at the joyous moments in your life. Imagine our Savior on the cross. Imagine Him on the right hand of the throne. Picture the King of Kings and Lord of Lords.

My Prayer

Week 2

Forging

Day 1

"O Nebuchadnezzar, we have no need to answer you in this matter. If that is the case, our God whom we serve is able to deliver us from the burning fiery furnace, and He will deliver us from your hand, O king. But if not, let it be known to you, O king, that we do not serve your gods, nor will we worship the gold image which you have set up."

Daniel 3:16-18

Recall a time when you were tested by the Lord. What feelings did you have during this time?

____

____

____

____

What did the testing produce in your life?

____

____

____

____

What new thing did you learn about yourself as a result of the test?

____

____

____

____

How does testing provide answers to question that were not asked?

How have your previous periods of testing shaped how you experience the presence of God?

How can you honor God during testing?

Tests are meant to evaluate not only the student but also the teacher. God is the master teacher. I am preparing for the next test. Today I am learning....

My Prayer

Day 2

For You have tried us, O God; You have refined us as silver is refined. You brought us into the net; You laid an oppressive burden upon our loins. You made men ride over our heads; We went through fire and through water, Yet You brought us out into a place of abundance.
Psalm 66:10-12

In what ways are you being tried?

____

____

____

____

How is your process of refinement like that of silver?

____

____

____

____

How does your refinement impact those around you?

____

____

____

____

How is your heart burdened? How can God utilize the burden to bring Himself glory?

____

____

____

____

List three benefits of being tried (tested, purified, refined) by fire.

1.______________________________________

____

____

____

2.______________________________________

____

____

____

3.______________________________________

____

____

____

When we go through the fire and the water God has a purpose for the process. Both the fire and the water are intentional. Your pain has a purpose and an end date.

My Prayer

Day 3

Therefore, they inquired further of the LORD, "Has the man come here yet?" So the LORD said, "Behold, he is hiding himself by the baggage."
Samuel 10:22

What has Lord shown you about your assignment during this season of refining?

____

____

____

____

In what ways are you inquiring of the Lord for confirmation, affirmation, and further instruction?

____

____

____

____

How have you chosen personal comfort over the will of God in your life?

____

____

____

____

What do you need to let go of in order to progress?

____

____

____

____

____

What are three things you can do today to come into agreement with God to move forward?

1.____

____

____

____

2.____

____

____

____

3.____

____

____

____

God stretches us beyond what we believe is possible. Moving forward requires dependence on God. Our calling is often in direct opposition to our personal comfort. Your submission is required.

My Prayer

Day 4

"And I will bring the third part through the fire, Refine them as silver is refined, And test them as gold is tested. They will call on My name, And I will answer them;I will say, 'They are My people,' And they will say, 'The Lord is my God.'"
Zechariah 13: 9

How can you continue to trust God in your refinement process?

____

____

____

____

In what area(s) are you being tested as gold is tested?

____

____

____

____

What are the benefits of being the "people of God"?

____

____

____

____

What are you calling out for in this season?

____

____

____

____

What questions in your life do you need answers?

____

____

____

____

How are you preparing yourself to revise the answers from God?

____

____

____

____

They will call on My name, And I will answer them; I will say, 'They are My people,' And they will say, 'The Lord is my God.'"

My Prayer

Day 5

Not that I speak from want, for I have learned to be content in whatever circumstances I am. I know how to get along with humble means, and I also know how to live in prosperity; in any and every circumstance I have learned the secret of being filled and going hungry, both of having abundance and suffering need.
Philippians 4:11-12

Define contentment?

____

____

____

____

In what areas do you have abundance in your relationship with God?

____

____

____

____

How are suffering for the sake of your relationship with God?

____

____

____

____

How is God using both your abundance and your lack during this time ?

____

____

____

____

How can you meet the needs of others when you are in a position of lack?

____

____

____

____

How is suffer Christ like?

____

____

____

____

Being grateful is a deliberate intentional choice. How are you deciding to be grateful ? How do you purpose in your heart to be grateful? In your prayer time today, write what you are grateful for to refocus your thoughts.

My Prayer

Day 6

... that they would seek God if perhaps they might grope for Him and find Him, though He is not far from each one of us; for in Him we live and move and exist, as even some of your own poets have said, 'For we also are His children.'

Acts 17:27-28

What spiritual disciplines do you practice when you feel far from God?

____

____

____

List three ways you are actively seeking God.

1.______________________________________

____

____

____

2.______________________________________

____

____

____

3.______________________________________

____

____

____

List three hinderances to your pursuit of God.

1.____

____

____

2.____

____

____

3.____

____

____

How does your lifestyle reflect that you are a child of God?

____

____

____

____

The more I seek you. The more I find you. As I find you, I become more aware of how present You are and how much I am loved. I am truly loved of God today and every day.

My Prayer

Day 7

My soul, wait in silence for God only, For my hope is from Him. He only is my rock and my salvation, My stronghold; I shall not be shaken. On God, my salvation and my glory rest; The rock of my strength, my refuge is in God. Trust in Him at all times, O people; Pour out your heart before Him; God is a refuge for us.
Psalm 62:5-8

What is your personal definition of refuge:

____

____

____

____

Where have you found refuge in the past?

____

____

____

____

What situation or circumstance has shaken you?

____

____

____

____

How has God provided refuge during this time?

How is refuge related to rest?

How is refuge related to trust?

Trust in Him at all times, O people; Pour out your heart before Him; God is a refuge for us... Nothing about us will cause God to reject us. Use this time to reflect on pouring out your whole heart to God.

My Prayer

Week 3
Annealing

Day 1

Unless the LORD builds the house,
They labor in vain who build it;
Unless the LORD guards the city,
The watchman keeps awake in vain.
Psalm 127:1

What are you building in this season?

____

____

____

____

What is more important to God quantity or quality? How can you support your answer?

____

____

____

____

How can you discern if you are building in vain?

____

____

____

____

When you build in vain what is the outcome?

____

____

____

____

What is the best way to honor God in your building?

____

____

____

____

How do you ensure that the Lord guards the what is being built?

____

____

____

____

The Lord desires to partner with us , journey with us and labor alongside us. To build anything without His approval, instruction and guidance is an exercise in futility.

My Prayer

Day 2

The LORD is my shepherd, I shall not want. He makes me lie down in green pastures; He leads me beside quiet waters. He restores my soul; He guides me in the paths of righteousness For His name's sake.
Psalm 23:1-3

How has the Lord been your shepherd?

____

____

____

____

Record a recent event where you felt lead by the Lord?

____

____

____

____

Recall the most recent time you rested in the presence of the Lord?

____

____

____

____

How is rest related to increased production?

____

____

____

____

How is rest related to growth or maturity?

____

____

____

____

What is the relationship between rest and restoration?

____

____

____

____

How is the Lord restoring you?

____

____

____

____

Culture often dictates how time is spent. God is not bound by culture. God is outside of culture, beyond culture and countercultural. Today I choose to follow the leading a guiding of the shepherd.

My Prayer

Day 3

Delight yourself in the Lord;
And He will give you the desires of your heart. Commit your way to the Lord, Trust also in Him, and He will do it. He will bring forth your righteousness as the light And your judgment as the noonday.
Rest in the Lord and wait patiently for Him...
Psalm 37: 4-7a

List three ways that you delight in the Lord.

*1.*____

____

____

____

*2.*____

____

____

____

*3.*____

____

____

____

In what areas are you committing yourself to the Lord?

____

____

____

____

What is your biggest obstacle in trusting the Lord?

____

____

____

____

How is patience related to righteousness?

____

____

____

____

It is challenging to be patient, wait and rest. Think of the faithfulness of God, reflect on the times you have delighted yourself in Him.

My Prayer

Day 4

I wait for the Lord, my soul does wait, And in His word do I hope.
My soul waits for the Lord. More than the watchmen for the morning; Indeed, more than the watchmen for the morning.
Psalm 130:5-6

Describe any reactions physical or spiritual that you have when waiting for an extended period.

____

____

____

____

Describe the difference between active and passive waiting?

____

____

____

____

Which type of waiting are you currently engaged?

____

____

____

____

Recall a time when "your soul waited for the Lord". How were you transformed by the waiting process?

____

____

____

____

What is God's responsibility in your life as the one who brings the morning?

____

____

____

____

How do you know God is trustworthy? Record evidence from your own life?

____

____

____

____

____

Waiting is a critical portion of refinement. Humanity struggles to wait with humility and patience. Focus on how you wait. Reflect on how waiting honors God.

My Prayer

Day 5

The Lord reigns forever; He has established His throne for judgment. He rules the world in righteousness and judges the peoples with equity. The Lord is a refuge for the oppressed, a stronghold in times of trouble. Those who know your name trust in you, for you, Lord, have never forsaken those who seek you.
Psalm 9:7-10

What personal examples reinforce that God Reigns in your life?

____

____

____

____

Describe a time when Gods was your refuge or stronghold?

____

____

____

____

Describe your level of trust in the Lord. How can you increase your trust in God's ability?

____

____

____

____

In what way are you seeking God as the righteous judge?

____

____

____

____

God is______________________________________.

God is a____________________________________.

God is my___________________________________.

God will____________________________________.

Think the names that you call God in your prayer time. Think of each of these names and reflect on how God has been each of these for you. Use this recognition to guide your prayer.

My Prayer

Day 6

My soul, wait in silence for God only, For my hope is from Him. He only is my rock and my salvation, My stronghold; I shall not be shaken. On God, my salvation and my glory rest; The rock of my strength, my refuge is in God. Trust in Him at all times, O people; Pour out your heart before Him; God is a refuge for us. Selah.

Psalm 62:5-12

How have you been shaken in your faith?

____

____

____

____

During times of hardship or seasons of shaking how has God been your Rock?

____

____

____

____

How is God your hope today?

____

____

____

____

How has God been your salvation?

____

____

____

____

How is God your glory rest?

____

____

____

____

What is the easiest way for you to pour out your heart to God?

____

____

____

____

Silence is often uncomfortable. Today take a few moments to quiet your mind. Be still and listen. Expect God to speak. What is the Lord saying? Record what the Lord is saying to you.

My Prayer

Day 7

The Lord is your keeper;The Lord is your shade on your right hand. The sun will not smite you by day, Nor the moon by night. The Lord will protect you from all evil;He will keep your soul. The Lord will guard your going out and your coming in. From this time forth and forever.

Psalm 121:5-8

List an example of how the Lord has been your keeper in the past.

____

____

____

____

How is the Lord your keeper today?

____

____

____

____

How have you witnessed the Lord's provision for you today?

____

____

____

____

What do you believe the Lord is protecting you from?

____

____

____

____

What evidence do you have that the Lord is journeying with you?

____

____

____

____

The Lord has promised to be the lover and keeper of your soul. How does this make you feel?

____

____

____

____

The promises of God are not to be taken lightly. The Lord has promised to be your protector , provider , your guard your salvation from this day and for all of eternity. Reflect on His goodness and mercy during your prayer time.

My Prayer

Week 4

Grinding

Day 1

But if you will seek God earnestly and plead with the Almighty ,if you are pure and upright, even now he will rouse himself on your behalf and restore you to your prosperous state. Your beginnings will seem humble, so prosperous will your future be.
Job 8:5-7

How have your perceptions of God been challenged in this season?

____

____

____

____

How have your perceptions of yourself been challenged during the season?

____

____

____

____

Define prosperity.

____

____

____

____

Define humility.

____

____

____

____

Define restoration.

____

____

____

____

How does prosperity and humility work together in the economy of God? Record a personal example.

____

____

____

____

____

Prosperity is a goal for many. Prosperity in the natural is a fluctuating state only in God can prosperity for a permanent state of being. We must agree and alignment ourselves with what God desires to truly walk in prosperity.

My Prayer

Day 2

But we have this treasure in earthen vessels, so that the surpassing greatness of the power will be of God and not from ourselves; we are afflicted in every way, but not crushed; perplexed, but not despairing; persecuted, but not forsaken; struck down, but not destroyed; always carrying about in the body the dying of Jesus, so that the life of Jesus also may be manifested in our body.
2 Corinthians 4: 7-10

How do you define yourself as a treasure?

____

____

____

____

How has affliction shaped you?

____

____

____

____

How is "pressure" transformative? Record examples from the natural world?

____

____

____

____

How is “pressure” transformative in your own life?

____

____

____

____

How is the cross an example of transformation?

____

____

____

____

How is the life of Jesus being manifested in your body?

____

____

____

____

____

The will of God in the process of refinement is to craft you not to destroy you. Do you trust Him to transform? Do you trust Him to create? Do you trust Him with your whole being? Let the answers move you to pray.

My Prayer

Day 3

Truly, truly, I say to you, unless a grain of wheat falls into the earth and dies, it remains alone; but if it dies, it bears much fruit. He who loves his life loses it, and he who hates his life in this world will keep it to life eternal.
John 24:12

List three things that you believe the Lord is challenging you to release in this season.

*1.*____

____

____

*2.*____

____

____

*3.*____

____

____

What do you have to resolve to release these things?

____

____

____

____

What do you see as your "seed"?

____

____

____

____

What fruit is being manifested as your seed chooses to die?

____

____

____

____

How is this fruit blessing others?

____

____

____

____

Jesus lived a life of sacrifice. The entirety of His ministry was focused on giving what He had unto others. The scriptures record that He had little reserved for Himself. This is the model that illustrates a willingness to give all that we have for the cause of Christ.

My Prayer

Day 4

Samuel said, "Has the Lord as much delight in burnt offerings and sacrifices As in obeying the voice of the Lord? Behold, to obey is better than sacrifice,
And to heed than the fat of rams.
Samuel 15:22

Define sacrifice:

____

____

____

____

Define obedience:

____

____

____

____

How is obedience a form of sacrifice?

____

____

____

____

When do you hear the voice of the Lord?

____

____

____

____

What is the Lord telling you to do?

____

____

____

____

What is keeping you from obeying?

____

____

____

____

Obedience implies there is a level of resistance. It will not always be an easy thing to follow the commands of the Lord. Be honest with God where you may be struggling to submit to His requirements.

My Prayer

Day 5

He who loves his life will lose it, and he who hates his life in this world will keep it for eternal life. If anyone serves Me, let him follow Me; and where I am, there My servant will be also. If anyone serves Me, him My Father will honor.

John 12:25-26

Define renovation:

___

___

___

___

___

Rate your willingness to lose your life?

___

___

___

___

Describe how the Lord is where you are?

___

___

___

___

How do you see the Lord using adversity to sharpen you during this season?

____

____

____

____

How are you committed to following the Lord?

____

____

____

____

How are you serving the Lord?

____

____

____

____

Be willing to lose everything to follow the path the Lord has laid out for you. Whatever the Lord requires of you He will give you the ability to release. Lord my prayer today is...

My Prayer

Day 6

"Do not be afraid," Samuel replied. "You have done all this evil; yet do not turn away from the Lord, but serve the Lord with all your heart. Do not turn away after useless idols. They can do you no good, nor can they rescue you, because they are useless. For the sake of his great name the Lord will not reject his people, because the Lord was pleased to make you his own.

1 Samuel 12:20-22

What areas in your life have you "turned away" from God?

____

____

____

____

List any idols you have erected in you life?

____

____

____

____

How can you turn back to God?

____

____

____

____

How are you serving the Lord not with actions but with your heart?

___

___

___

___

How do you know the Lord will not reject you?

___

___

___

___

How many times will the Lord receive your repentance?

___

___

___

___

___

Remember that the Lord has not rejected you! You are being pursued. You are desired. No matter the choices of your past remember the Lord still loves you.

My Prayer

Day 7

For I am convinced that neither death, nor life, nor angels, nor principalities, nor things present, nor things to come, nor powers, nor height, nor depth, nor any other created thing, will be able to separate us from the love of God, which is in Christ Jesus our Lord.

Romans 8:37-39

What behaviors do you think can separate you from the love of God?

____

____

____

____

What created things do you believe can separate you from the love of God?

____

____

____

____

Where do you see God's grace at work in your life?

____

____

____

____

How can God affirm His love for you?

____

____

____

____

How do you feel you the love of God?

____

____

____

____

You will always be victorious. You will win because the God of the universe does not lie, and the God of the universe promised you would.

My Prayer

Week 5

Hardening

Day 1

Let your eyes look directly ahead and let your gaze be fixed straight in front of you. Watch the path of your feet
And all your ways will be established. Do not turn to the right nor to the left; Turn your foot from evil.

Proverbs 4:25-27

What is your focus today?

____

____

____

____

What types of activities help you to stay focused and "watch your feet"?

____

____

____

____

Who or what tends to distract you?

____

____

____

____

How do you know when you have become distracted?

____

____

____

____

List ways that you can partner with God to establish His ways in your life.

____

____

____

____

____

There are many distractions. We are often encumbered by many things. Use this time to settle you mind and focus on how the Lord has called to focus on Him.

My Prayer

Day 2

The spirit of a man can endure his sickness, but as for a broken spirit who can bear it? The mind of the prudent acquires knowledge, and the ear of the wise seeks knowledge. A man's gift makes room for him and brings him before great men.

Proverbs 18:14-16

How are your thoughts connected to the way you feel?

____

____

____

____

Why is it prudent to acquire knowledge?

____

____

____

____

What are you listening to that promotes the acquisition of knowledge?

____

____

____

____

What are the gifts the Lord placed in your hands?

How are you becoming trustworthy with your gifts?

In what ways is the Lord making room for you?

The way that we think has a tremendous impact on how we feel, our motivation and our ability to accomplish our goals. God is beginning to challenge the way you think to prepare you for expansion. Ask the Lord to help you renew your mind and transform your thinking.

My Prayer

Day 3

The plans of the heart belong to man,
But the answer of the tongue is from the Lord.
All the ways of a man are clean in his own sight,
But the Lord weighs the motives. Commit your works to the Lord
And your plans will be established.
Proverbs 16:1-3

How have your plans differed from God's plans for your life?

____

____

____

____

How have your motives been challenged by the Lord?

____

____

____

____

How are you reconciling what you want versus what God wants during this time?

____

____

____

____

Which current plans to you need to submit to the Lord for evaluation ?

____

____

____

____

____

In what new way can you commit your way to the Lord?

____

____

____

____

____

God's plan for His children are bigger than what can be accomplished in one's own strength. Knowing this is humbling. Take a moment to commit your way to the Lord being honest where your understanding is limited.

My Prayer

Day 4

Do not love sleep or you will grow poor; stay awake and you will have food to spare. "It's no good, it's no good!" says the buyer—then goes off and boasts about the purchase. Gold there is, and rubies in abundance, but lips that speak knowledge are a rare jewel.

Proverbs 20:13-16

Define procrastination:

____

____

____

____

How is procrastination related to lack in the scripture?

____

____

____

____

____

In what ways are you trying to stay awake?

____

____

____

____

____

What things can potentially lull you to sleep?

____

____

____

____

How does knowledge produce abundance?

____

____

____

____

In what area do you desire to have more knowledge?

____

____

____

____

It is easy to become avoidant when there is much you need to accomplish. Staying still will not accomplish much but neither will busyness. Ask the Lord to give you the knowledge and strategy to advance His works in your life.

My Prayer

Day 5

One who is gracious to a poor man lends to the LORD, And He will repay him for his good deed.

Proverbs 19:17

Define the principle of sowing and reaping in God's economy?

____

____

____

____

How do you see this principle at work in your life?

____

____

____

____

How can you purpose in your heart to give more freely?

____

____

____

____

What can you lend to others that is not monetary?

____

____

____

____

How do you feel when you give with no expectation of return?

____

____

____

____

How has God repaid you for sacrificial giving?

____

____

____

____

God is the One that is responsible for payment of good deeds! God is the one who can measure the gift's true value, but God also measures the heart of the person giving the gift. Ask the Lord to measure your heart in your prayer today.

My Prayer

Day 6

The naive believes everything, But the sensible man considers his steps. A wise man is cautious and turns away from evil, But a fool is arrogant and careless. The naive inherit foolishness, But the sensible are crowned with knowledge.

Proverbs 14:15-16, 18

What process do you use to consider your steps?

____

____

____

____

How are the terms sensible, cautious and wise related?

____

____

____

____

How do you combat foolishness in your practices and in your thinking?

____

____

____

____

How are foolishness and arrogance related?

____

____

____

____

How is humility related to knowledge?

____

____

____

____

What legacy are you leaving ? What can others inherit from you?

____

____

____

____

Human knowledge is vastly different then wisdom and knowledge granted by the Lord. The Lord desires to grant you insight into His plans be humble enough to receive it.

My Prayer

Day 7

Get wisdom, get understanding: forget it not; neither decline from the words of my mouth. Forsake her not, and she shall preserve thee: love her, and she shall keep thee. Wisdom is the principal thing; therefore, get wisdom: and with all thy getting get understanding.

Proverbs 4:5-7

Define Wisdom as a person:

____

____

____

____

Define wisdom as a concept?

____

____

____

____

How can acquire wisdom yet lack understanding?

____

____

____

____

How is wisdom applied knowledge?

____

____

____

____

How can you multiply wisdom?

____

____

____

____

How do you share what you have learned with others?

____

____

____

____

In all your getting get understanding. When you lack anything your source is the Lord.

My Prayer

Week 6
Tempering

Day 1

Beloved, let us love one another, for love is from God, and everyone who loves is born of God and knows God. The one who does not love does not know God, for God is love.

1 John 4:7-8

Love is...

____

____

____

____

Love feels...

____

____

____

____

Love requires...

____

____

____

____

I love...

___

___

___

___

I am loved by...

___

___

___

___

Love is a choice. Love is a mandate. Love is required. Love is not always reciprocal but the one who does not love does not know God, for God is love.

My Prayer

Day 2

Be completely humble and gentle; be patient, bearing with one another in love. Make every effort to keep the unity of the Spirit through the bond of peace. There is one body and one Spirit, just as you were called to one hope when you were called; one Lord, one faith, one baptism; one God and Father of all, who is over all and through all and in all.

Ephesians 4:2-6

How do you typically bare others in love?

____

____

____

____

Do you find this easy or difficult?

____

____

____

____

What efforts are you making to keep the unity of the Spirit?

____

____

____

____

How do you respond to disunity in your relationships?

____

____

____

____

How does cohesion and unity honor God?

____

____

____

____

____

What can you do to increase unity in the Body of Christ?

____

____

____

____

Make every effort to keep the unity of the Spirit through the bond of peace. Unity fosters the love of God.

My Prayer

Day 3

Therefore, as God's chosen people, holy and dearly loved, clothe yourselves with compassion, kindness, humility, gentleness and patience. Bear with each other and forgive one another if any of you has a grievance against someone. Forgive as the Lord forgave you.

Colossians 3:12-13

What does it mean to clothe one's self with compassion, kindness and humility?

____

____

____

____

How is compassion related to forgiveness?

____

____

____

____

List offenses that you have refused to forgive.

____

____

____

____

List actions you have refused to forgive yourself.

How is Christ's forgiveness of our sins a mandate to forgive our offenders ?

Forgiveness like love is a choice that we must willingly grant. God requires us to forgive others as He has forgiven us. This is a task that is not easy, but it is possible.

My Prayer

Day 4

Above all, keep fervent in your love for one another, because love covers a multitude of sins. Be hospitable to one another without complaint. As each one has received a special gift, employ it in serving one another as good stewards of the manifold grace of God.

1 Peter 4:8-10

Describe fervent love.

____

____

____

____

Love covers a multitude of sins; how do you see this principle operating in your life?

____

____

____

____

What can you do to avoid being inhospitable to those who have offended you?

____

____

____

____

What special gifts have you been given to share?

____

____

____

____

____

How do you become a steward of God's grace?

____

____

____

____

Being a steward of God's manifold grace is a privilege and a responsibility. Reflect on His choice of you to carry out this mission.

My Prayer

Day 5

"The Lord did not set His love on you nor choose you because you were more in number than any of the peoples, for you were the fewest of all peoples, but because the Lord loved you ... Know therefore that the Lord your God, He is God, the faithful God, who keeps His covenant and His lovingkindness to a thousandth generation with those who love Him and keep His commandments.

Deuteronomy 7:7-8a,9

The Lord chose to love you before you could ever choose to love him back. How does this make you feel?

____

____

____

____

____

God is faithful even when we are faithless. How does this make you feel?

____

____

____

____

____

How do you thank God for his faithfulness?

____

____

____

____

How does your care and treatment of others mirror God's care and treatment of you?

____

____

____

____

How can you purpose in your heart to love others more intently by forgiving offense?

____

____

____

____

You did not have to earn or qualify for God's love for you. It is then not equitable to make others earn or qualify for them to be loved by you.

My Prayer

Day 6

The weapons we fight with are not the weapons of the world. On the contrary, they have divine power to demolish strongholds. We demolish arguments and every pretension that sets itself up against the knowledge of God, and we take captive every thought to make it obedient to Christ.

2Cor. 10:4-5

What are the weapons with which we fight?

____

____

____

____

What are the weapons of the world?

____

____

____

____

Define carnality:

____

____

____

____

How does the carnal mind respond to the knowledge of God?

____

____

____

____

How does the refined mind respond to the knowledge of God?

____

____

____

____

The way that God fights battles is dramatically different from the way we fight battles in our humanity. The Lord can show us how to war in a way that puts only sin to death.

My Prayer

Day 7

Beloved, let us love one another, for love is from God; and everyone who loves is born of God and knows God. The one who does not love does not know God, for God is love.

1 John 4:7-8

Complete the following acrostic

G_______________________________.

O_______________________________.

D_______________________________.

I_______________________________.

S_______________________________.

L_______________________________.

O_______________________________.

V_______________________________.

E_______________________________.

Love is from God so I will...

____

____

____

____

I am born of God, I show love by...

____

____

____

____

God is love which causes me to...

____

____

____

____

God has decreed that we are born of Him. He has affirmed that He is love! Mediate on his love, let His love wash over you , rest knowing that love His love is the foundation of His character and He can not deny Himself.

My Prayer

Week 7
Completion

Day 1

Such confidence we have through Christ toward God. Not that we are adequate in ourselves to consider anything as coming from ourselves, but our adequacy is from God, who also made us adequate as servants of a new covenant, not of the letter but of the Spirit; for the letter kills, but the Spirit gives life.
2 Corinthians 3

What inadequacies do you ruminate on daily?

____

____

____

____

How do you receive God's affirmation?

____

____

____

____

In what type of environment do I excel?

____

____

____

____

What are some qualities do you have which are valuable or useful to God?

____

____

____

____

Are there any areas in my life where I feel out of place or disjointed?

____

____

____

____

Am I walking in the direction of God’s plan?

____

____

____

____

The letter kills but the Spirit gives life!

My Prayer

Day 2

Therefore let us draw near with confidence to the throne of grace, so that we may receive mercy and find grace to help in time of need.

Hebrews 4:16

Have there been times when you have told yourself that you are not valuable?

____

____

____

____

How have you been impacted by God's grace and mercy?

____

____

____

____

How can you increase your confidence in God?

____

____

____

____

How can you increase your confidence in yourself ?

___

___

___

___

Confidence can be cultivated with intention. Confidence is built up from consistent encounters with similar outcomes. But most importantly knowing who you are in God.

My Prayer

Day 3

For just as the sufferings of Christ are ours in abundance, so also our comfort is abundant through Christ. But if we are afflicted, it is for your comfort and salvation; or if we are comforted, it is for your comfort, which is effective in the patient enduring of the same sufferings which we also suffer; and our hope for you is firmly grounded, knowing that as you are sharers of our sufferings, so also you are sharers of our comfort.

2 Corinthians 1:5-7

What feelings are most present for you today?

____

____

____

____

Are your feeling aligned with the Word of God for you?

____

____

____

____

How can you use your present spiritual process to help others?

____

____

____

____

How is pain beneficial to your growth and development?

____

____

____

____

How have you been hindered in your refinement process and how can you now begin to move forward?

____

____

____

____

Growth often requires persistence and endurance in the face of pain. Discomfort is not a sign of weakness it is a sign of strength being tested and extended. Your pain is producing something valuable in you.

My Prayer

Day 4

Or what man is there among you who, when his son asks for a loaf, will give him a stone? Or [if he asks for a fish, he will not give him a snake, will he? [11] If you then, being evil, know how to give good gifts to your children, how much more will your Father who is in heaven give what is good to those who ask Him!

Matthew7:9-11

How is trust related to yielding to the will of God?

____

____

____

____

How do you remind yourself that God's plan is good for you?

____

____

____

____

Where do you see the most growth happening right now?

____

____

____

____

How can you be more open to the “grinding” process?

____

____

____

____

Lord, thank You for the grinding, the striping and the sharpening! While it may not feel good, it is not only good, it is essential.

My Prayer

Day 5

The LORD is my light and my salvation— whom shall I fear? The LORD is the stronghold of my life— of whom shall I be afraid? When the wicked advance against me to devour me, it is my enemies and my foes who will stumble and fall. Though an army besiege me, my heart will not fear; though war break out against me, even then I will be confident.
Psalm 27:1-3

List any remaining fears you have in your process of refinement.

____

____

____

____

How is God affirming your ability to "fear not"?

____

____

____

____

How does the adversary use fear to stagnate?

____

____

____

____

Where do see victory in your process?

____

____

____

____

How can you denounce fear and move forward?

____

____

____

____

Fear is not of God so I will trust instead! The Lord has given you every reason to trust Him . Be attentive to what He is leading you to do in this season reflect on His goodness, His grace and His mercy.

My Prayer

Day 6

To this end also we pray for you always, that our God will count you worthy of your calling, and fulfill every desire for goodness and the work of faith with power, so that the name of our Lord Jesus will be glorified in you, and you in Him, according to the grace of our God and the Lord Jesus Christ.

2 Thessalonians1:11-12

How are becoming worthy or your calling?

____

____

____

____

How are you desiring goodness and how can you multiply goodness in your environment?

____

____

____

____

How do you describe the grace of God?

____

____

____

____

In what areas do you see the Lord working in faith and power in your life?

____

____

____

____

How is the Lord glorified in you?

____

____

____

____

As you seek the things of God the kingdom of God and His plans and purposes know that He is with you He is in your corner. Use your prayer time to align yourself with Him.

My Prayer

Day 7

His master said to him, 'Well done, good and faithful servant. You were faithful with a few things, I will put you in charge of many things; enter into the joy of your master.'
Matthew 25:21

What has the Lord said to you about your life?

____

____

____

____

What are you doing to multiply the gifts that you have been given ?

____

____

____

____

How are you being diligent in your walk with the Lord?

____

____

____

____

What are you taking with you from your guided time with Him?

____

____

____

____

What are your next steps in spiritual refinement ?

____

____

____

____

The journey of refinement is not about completing any one goal. Refinement is about being in the best position to live the life God has planned out and crafted for you in His divine will. It is to strive to hear 'Well done, good and faithful servant. You were faithful with a few things, I will put you in charge of many things; enter into the joy of your master.'

My Prayer